It's Hard Not to Worry

Stories for Children About Poverty

John M. Barrett

Illustrations by
Davis Hannah

FRIENDSHIP PRESS • NEW YORK

Library of Congress Cataloging-in-Publication Data

Barrett, John M.
It's hard not to worry.

Includes bibliographical references.
Summary: A collection of six stories with Christian emphasis about North American children whose families are facing or living in poverty. Includes discussion guide.
1. Poverty—Religious aspects—Christianity—Juvenile literature. [1. Poverty—Religious aspects—Christianity. 2. Christian life] I. Hannah, Davis, ill. II. Title.
BV639.P6B37 1988 261.8'325 87-37521
ISBN 0-377-00178-3

ISBN: 0-377-00178-3
Editorial Offices: Room 722, 475 Riverside Drive, New York, NY 10115
Distribution Offices: P.O. Box 37844, Cincinnati, OH 45237

Printed in the United States of America

TABLE OF CONTENTS

It's Hard Not to Worry

I could tell that something was wrong, that something bad was going to happen, long before that awful day.

Mom and Dad talked about it all the time, not just after I went to bed. There were words I didn't understand, like "contracts" and "pink slips" and "no benefits." And lots of questions without answers: "I don't know what we'll do. How will we pay the bills? Where can we go?"

But whenever I tried to find out what was going on, they just said, "Oh, never mind, Joey, honey. There's nothing for you to worry about." Then they would change the subject, and start to talk about my homework or something else that wasn't very important.

That's one thing I don't like about adults. They think that kids are little babies, that we don't know anything. They try to protect us too much, and that makes everything worse. We worry more.

I'm the oldest child in our family. I'm nine. My little brother and sister are five-year-old twins. They really are too young to know much, and they live in a little kindergarten world of their own anyway. So, I'm stuck, all alone, trying to figure everything out for myself.

I really started worrying yesterday when Dad came home from work. Dad's job is closer to our house than Mom's job, so he comes home first. Rusty, our dog, knows the sound of the car, so he rushed to the door like he always does, and I followed him. The car turned into the driveway much faster than usual. I heard the tires squeal and then a loud crack. The twins' toy trucks had been sitting in the driveway, right in the path of the car.

Dad jumped out of the car and slammed the door. "How many times have I told you kids not to leave your toys in the driveway!" he shouted. My dad is great at making jokes by pretending to be upset, but this didn't sound like a joke. Well, the kids *were* stupid to leave their good trucks out there, but they are pretty little to do everything right, and Dad had been driving too fast.

The twins had run out for a hug, but when they heard the tone of Dad's voice they ran right back, to their favorite hiding place under the big pine tree by the fence. Thank goodness I had remembered to put my bike where it belonged!

Every day when Dad gets home, he starts getting dinner ready, and I help. We usually have fun cooking together, or doing whatever we do. But after what happened outside, it didn't look like fixing dinner was going to be any treat. When Dad walked into the kitchen, he didn't smile at me or want to cook or wrestle or anything. He just sat down and said, "Go away. Leave me alone."

Rusty had come up to Dad to be petted and have his ears rubbed. But tonight Dad even pushed Rusty away, saying, "I'm sick of that dog, too. Get him out of here."

For a long time I'd been getting worried that maybe I had done something that was making Dad upset. But for days and days I had been extra careful—putting my bike away, setting my alarm clock so I would be sure to be ready for the school bus, not even yelling too much when the twins got into my room and messed up my stuff. I couldn't think of anything really bad that I'd done.

Now, when Dad told me to leave him alone, I ran to my room and jumped on my bed and started to cry. Rusty followed me and jumped up on the bed too.

When Mom came home, she and Dad started talking so softly that I couldn't hear what they were saying. I was trying not to care what they said, but that was hard to do.

I think I was almost asleep when I heard a little knock on my bedroom door, and Dad and Mom came into the room.

"Joe, how are you feeling?" Mom asked. "You're never in bed when I come home from work unless you're sick."

"I'm OK," I answered. "No, I'm not OK. I don't know how I am. I'm mixed-up. Nothing's the same. I'm afraid I did something wrong, but I don't know what it is. Nobody tells me anything, and Dad doesn't like me anymore!" I turned my head to the wall and didn't look at them.

I could feel Mom and Dad sit down on the bed. Then Dad put his big hand on my shoulder and started to squeeze it softly, like he used to. Maybe he still liked me after all.

"Look at me, Joe," he said.

I rolled over and looked at him and at Mom too.

"I'm sorry, Joe," Dad said. "I haven't been myself lately. It's not your fault that I'm angry. You see, the factory is closing. We found out today for sure. That means that in a few months none of the people who work there will have a job. We're all upset with the company, but there doesn't seem to be anything that I or anyone else can do. I thought I would work there and make cars all my life, like Grandpa. Now I feel like I've let your Mom and you and the twins down. That's why I was so mad when I came home. It's not your fault, or the twins' fault either. I'm sorry."

"Gee, Dad, I didn't know all that," I said. "I've got my birthday money in the bank. Maybe we can buy the factory and you all can keep your jobs!"

Mom smiled. "That would cost millions of dollars, Joe, but it's a thoughtful idea. Dad's going to find a new job. We might even move to a new town."

"I want to stay here," I said, sticking out my lower lip. "This is home. I don't want any other town."

"We'll have to see, Joey," Dad said. "We don't always get what we want. But we'll try to do a better job of letting you know what's going on. And there's something else we can do too. We can pray to God about it."

"Wait a minute!" I said. "Why did God let this happen, anyway? We pray every night. Why didn't God keep the factory open?"

"God doesn't protect us from problems," Mom said.

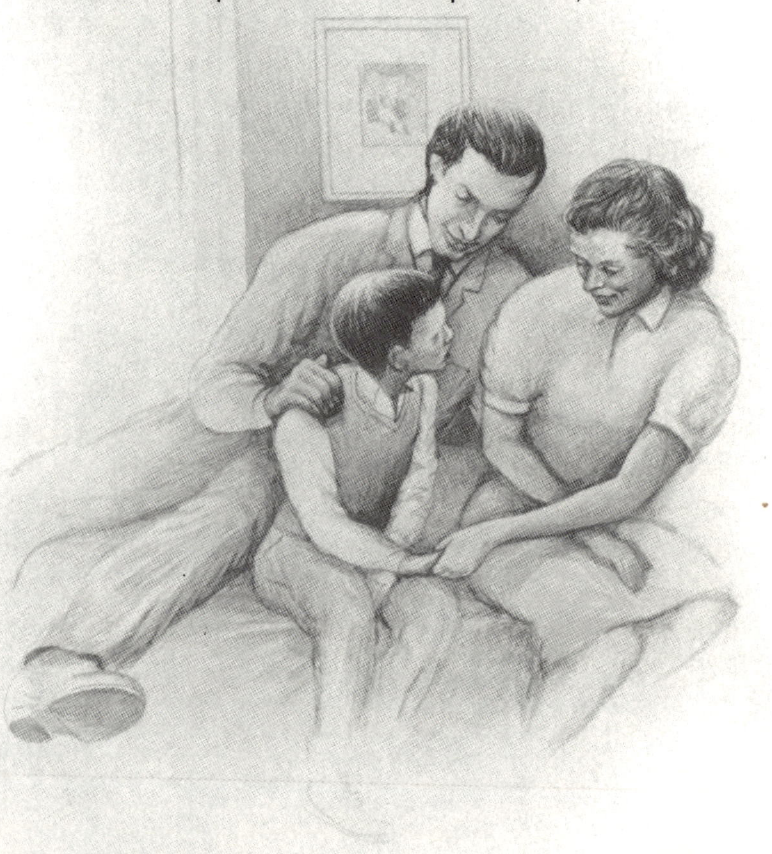

"Everyone has problems—Jesus did too. Remember when his friends, the disciples, ran away from him the night before he died?"

"Yes, but then, if we still have all our problems, how does God help us?" I asked.

"Well," Dad said, "God loves us, and this love gives us the strength and faith to face our problems and go on with our lives."

"Do you remember what Jesus said about the lilies?" Mom asked.*

"No," I answered.

"That's where Jesus tells us not to worry," Mom said. "Because God will take care of us, like God takes care of the flowers and birds."

"Yes," Dad said. "But we have to do some things too, like loving God and others. When we trust God, then we don't worry so much, and God helps us find what we need for our lives."

"Even a new job?" I asked.

"I hope so," Dad answered, sighing, "and I believe so, but things may be tough for all of us for a while."

"I've got the Bible that the church gave me," I said. "Could we read that part about the lilies? Maybe that would help."

"That's a good idea!" Mom said.

I ran to my bookcase and got my Bible. Then I sat between my parents on the bed. We found the right place together, and I started reading.

"Therefore I tell you, do not be anxious (or worry) about your life...."

My parents each put an arm around me, and for the first time in a long time, I did not feel worried at all.

---

* What Jesus said about the lilies is in Matthew 6:25-34.

A Discussion and Action Guide for Families

1. Why was Joe so worried?
2. What did he imagine the problem to be? What was the real problem? Which was worse to Joe?
3. Ask all your family members what they are worried about. Maybe some insight and facts from one another will help reduce their worries.
4. Discuss how your faith in God has helped you with your problems in the past. Think of ways to let God reach and help you now, such as going to church, reading the Bible together, praying and helping others.
5. Read and discuss Matthew 6:25-34, a part of the Sermon on the Mount where Jesus teaches about trusting in God. Talk about God's love for us, how we experience it in church and daily life, and how we share this love with others.
6. Find out what your church is doing to help people without jobs. What can your family do to help?

Sara's Choice

Sara woke up early the day before the big sale. This was the last day that their farm and the land and the animals would still belong to her family. Tomorrow morning, hundreds of people would come to buy almost everything they owned.

These auction sales had already happened to some of Sara's friends, so she knew what to expect. Still, she couldn't exactly believe that after tomorrow Maple Grove Farm would no longer be her home. She had lived there her whole life—every one of her eleven years. She knew the red barn and almost every tree and field by heart.

Sara rolled over onto her side and tried to go back to sleep. She wanted to wake up and have the auction sale be a bad dream that would disappear like the morning mist in the meadow.

Sara tried to fall asleep, but she heard her parents in the kitchen. Life on a farm starts before dawn, even on the last day. She got dressed and went downstairs.

"Hi, honey," her mother greeted her.

"Morning, Mom," Sara answered. "Where's Dad?"

"Out in the barn, of course," her mother said. "Your dad will always be a farmer, even when we leave this

place tomorrow and move to town."

"Are you sure they'll have the sale, Mom?" Sara asked for the hundredth time. "How can they sell our farm? It's ours. We've planted our crops and taken care of the animals, every day, even on Sundays. It isn't fair! It isn't! It isn't!"

Sara's mother came around behind her and put an arm over Sara's shoulder. Sara could tell that her mother didn't want Sara to see the tears in her eyes. But by her mother's voice, Sara could tell that she had been crying.

"I know, dear," her mother said. "It isn't fair. We've all worked very hard. But we also borrowed money from the bank to pay for the new tractor and harvester. We borrowed more for seed and fertilizer. With bad weather and bad prices for our crops, we haven't been able to pay enough back."

"So they're taking everything we have?" Sara asked again. "Why can't they wait until next year?"

"They say they can't give us any more time. It breaks my heart and your father's, too. But at least we'll have a place to live in town. And Dad has a job," her mother said. "I'll get one myself, once we're settled."

"You can do what you want, Mom," Sara said. "I'm not going—and I'm not selling Belle, either. I raised her since she was born. She's mine."

Sara's mother was quiet for a moment. Then she turned Sara around and looked at her. "You have to go with us, Sara," her mother said. "But what you do with Belle is up to you. She's yours. That's a fact."

"I'm going out to see her," Sara said, running from the room.

Sara didn't see her father in the barn. She went right to Belle's stall. The little calf greeted her with a smile and a lick on the hand. Her brown-and-white-spotted face made her look like a friendly clown.

"Nobody will break us apart, Belle," Sara said, stroking Belle's nose. Sara's eyes filled with tears, and she hugged the young animal around its neck.

"Mom and Dad don't care about us any more," Sara said. "They want a new life. They say things will be better. But they won't be, not for me, and not for you."

Just then Sara heard a noise. She turned and saw her father standing in the doorway. He walked up to her, and they hugged each other.

"Sara," he said, "I couldn't help overhearing. You know, I don't really want a new life. I love farming, and I love this farm. But I've done all I can do and I'm tired. Your mom and you have worked as hard as you can, too. So—a new life is all we have. It's what God is giving us right now. We have to try to be thankful—somehow, in spite of everything else we're feeling."

"Thankful?" Sara snorted. "For what?"

"Well," he said, "we have our health, and each other, our church and friends, and a fresh start, not too far from here. We have God's love too, wherever we go."

"If God loves us, why didn't God answer my prayers and make us rich—so we could pay the bank and keep our farm?"

"God doesn't care about those kinds of riches," her father said. "Let me tell you a story that Jesus once told about money.*

"Once Jesus saw rich people putting gold coins into the offering. Those coins must have been worth twenty dollars, at least. Then a poor person put in two copper coins—probably worth about a penny or two. Jesus said that the poor person gave more than all the others, because she gave all that she had. The offerings of the rich meant little to them because they had so much. But the poor person had the love and faith to give her only two coins to God. Jesus understood true riches, and we must try to do the same."

---

* The story Jesus told about money is in Mark 12:41-44

FARM
AUCTION
TODAY

Sara looked down at the ground. "I don't want to be rich," she said. "I just love Belle, and I hate selling her."

"Do you want to give Belle away?" her father asked. "She's yours, so the bank doesn't have a claim on her."

"No, Dad," Sara said. "That wouldn't be fair to you and Mom. I want to do my part to help, but it's not easy to say good-bye."

"I know," her father said. "It's very hard."

"But I have to do it," Sara said. "We'll all be saying good-bye to what we've loved here."

"We'll always have our memories, Sara," Dad said, "and we'll be adding new memories every day."

Just then Sara's mother came in.

"Guess what?" Sara said. "I'm OK. I'm—I'm going to sell Belle. Maybe someday I can visit her. Dad helped me understand what's most important. Now I know—it's love and faith and our family."

"I'm proud of you, Sara," each of her parents said, at almost the same time.

"Maybe you'd like to take one of the new kittens with us," her mother said.

"You could even call it Belle," her father suggested.

"No, Dad," Sara said. "There will only be one Belle, ever, for me. But maybe I could call her Anna—Annabelle. That would be nice. But right now I've got chores to do. This is still a farm, isn't it?"

"It sure is," her parents agreed.

They hugged each other for a long time and then went to do their last regular day of chores. They all had tears in their eyes, but they all were smiling too, for they knew that this was the day that the Lord had made, and there would be a new tomorrow.

A Discussion and Action Guide for Families

1. Why does Sara's family have to sell almost everything they own?
2. Why is Sara especially upset? What makes her start to feel a little better?
3. How do you think your family would feel about having to sell everything you own and begin again? What might make this a positive, fresh start?
4. Being a family means experiencing both good and bad times, and helping one another. How have you helped each other lately?
5. If farms in your area are being sold at auction, how can you and your church be of help to those families? Ask your church's mission committee or your minister what your denomination is doing for farm families. See what your congregation can do to help.
6. Read and discuss Mark 12:41-44. Why doesn't the large offering impress Jesus? Why do you think the poor woman put all that she had into the offering? What were her riches? Whom was she trusting?

Surprise!

I usually sleep late on Saturday morning—until nine or ten o'clock. It's the one day I don't have to get up for school or church. Mama has to go to work early on Saturday, like she does on weekdays. So I get stuck taking care of my little sisters, Yvette and Glynda. If I'm still asleep, they have to be real quiet, and they usually are. They're all right, for being little kids. They don't give me much trouble.

I really don't like taking care of them every single Saturday, but there's not much I can do about it. You see, I'm the man of the house. I don't have a father, at least not one that I know and who knows me.

My father left after Glynda was born, seven years ago. I was only four then, and Yvette was two. He left to go back South. He said he'd send for us, but we never heard from him again. I still hope he'll come back someday, but I don't tell Mama. She gets angry when I talk that way about him.

If he'd come back, things would be different. We'd have two people earning money, and maybe we could get a bigger apartment. I'd like to have my own room, instead of sharing one with my sisters. We never have money to go to pizza or hamburger places like you see on television.

Maybe I'll get a job soon, and then we won't need food stamps and free breakfasts and lunches, and everything else that says we're poor.

Anyway, I got up early today because it's a special day, and I was expecting something special to happen. The girls were still asleep, and I walked real quiet so I wouldn't wake them.

Mama was still in the kitchen having coffee when I walked in.

"Why, Taylor," she said, "I didn't hear any earthquake. What are you doing up so early on Saturday? You sick or something?"

"No, Mama," I answered. "I just wanted to get up and see you before you went to work."

"Taylor," Mama said, "if you're wanting money, I don't have an extra dime or nothing. I wish I did. I wish I could pay you for all you do to help me."

"I don't want money, Mama, not today. I was expecting something, though—something all wrapped up—all fancy. You know," I said.

"What are you saying, Taylor? Don't talk nonsense. I've got to go to work in five minutes," Mama said.

I turned from her and looked out the window at the building next door.

"If you don't know what today is, Mama, I'm not going to tell you," I said.

Mama was quiet and then she said, "Taylor, it's Saturday, February 11th—no—it's February 12th. So? Oh, Taylor! Come here, boy. How could I forget? It's your birthday. Happy birthday, my man, my eleven-year-old man."

I went over to her, and we hugged. I didn't know what to think. It didn't look like I'd be getting any present, if she didn't even know it was my birthday.

"I'm sorry, Taylor," she said. "Working two jobs made me lose track of the days and months. I couldn't save anything with all the bills for January and February. I don't have anything for you—not even a cake. Let's have your birthday next month. It'll be better. I promise. I've got to go, Taylor. If I'm late I lose a half-hour's pay. Go back to bed. I'll be home around seven. Get the beans started. Taylor, I'm sorry."

We hugged again, and without really looking at her I said, "Don't worry, Mama. I don't care. It's just another Saturday, just another day. It doesn't matter."

"Thanks, son," she said. "Good-bye. Be good."

I went back to the bedroom and lay down. My eyes filled with tears as I realized I would not be getting the radio or jacket I'd been wishing for. I bit my lip and said under my breath, "I don't believe in wishes. I don't believe in them! They never come true. They never come true for me."

I rolled over on my stomach and closed my eyes. I thought I was dreaming when I heard voices in each ear saying, "Taylor, Taylor, it's noon. Won't you ever get up? We're tired of being quiet!"

I growled and grabbed a sister with each arm. "Now, my pretties," I said, "it's time for breakfast."

"No," they shouted. "It's time for lunch."

"And all we have," Yvette said, "is one piece of bread and a little grape jelly."

"I'll go to the store," I said, getting up. "I have almost a dollar from collecting soda cans. I'll buy some bread and honey. I should have enough. I'll get dressed right now."

I was ready in no time. "Be good," I said. "Don't open the door, unless it's me."

I was feeling good, feeling in charge, walking down the stairs, and then I remembered. This wasn't just any Saturday. It was my birthday, and there wasn't going to be any present or party. Not even a birthday cake. I kicked the wall, but I hurt my foot more than I did the wall.

"Ouch! Blast it!" I yelled at myself.

I walked into the supermarket and went to the bargain section with the stuff slightly older than fresh. I hated the section, but the prices were right. Mama had taught me how to check the date so the food wasn't *too* old. I found some bread for thirty-three cents. The honey was too expensive, but I found some more grape jelly for sixty cents. That would about finish my soda can money, with nothing left over for me. I had thought I would use the money to buy some birthday candles for my cake, but now there wasn't going to be any cake, until next month or next year.

Walking through the store, I was feeling pretty sorry for myself. Most people had full grocery carts and would be having big meals and parties. But not our family, never us. No matter how hard we worked or how good I was, there was never enough food or money.

I reached up and put my hand on a package of two chocolate cupcakes. They cost a lot. I couldn't get them and the bread and jelly too.

I kept my hand on the cupcakes. I looked up and down the aisle. Nobody was in sight. I slipped the cupcakes into my jacket. I had never stolen anything before, but

SHOP · MART

it was my birthday. I deserved a cake. Even cupcakes would be better than nothing.

I turned around, and felt a hand on each shoulder.

"Uh, oh," I said, while my stomach hit the floor.

I looked up into the smiling face of a friend from church, Michael Greene. I felt a lot better.

"Hey, Michael. How's it going?" I asked.

"Pretty good," Michael answered. "But what's that in your jacket, my friend? It's not cool to take stuff. It's not worth it, and it's not right."

I reached into my jacket and pulled out the cupcakes. They didn't look so good to me anymore.

"Michael," I said, "I didn't want to steal them. It just happened. It's my birthday. Mama forgot. I'm not getting a present, a cake or anything. It was wrong, but I was feeling bad and mixed-up, I guess. I'm sorry."

Michael squeezed my shoulders. He was smiling now.

"Put them back," he said. "They're no good anyway. I'm going to make you a cake, a real birthday cake. I never made one before, but I feel hot today. And the only thing I want to see in that jacket is you. Understand?"

"Yes," I said, "but I don't have enough money to buy all the cake stuff."

"I'm buying it," he said. "It's a present. I just got paid yesterday, and I'd like to spend some of it on you."

"But why do you want to spend your money on me?" I said. "You've got things to buy for yourself."

"Look, my friend," Michael said, serious now. "I've been where you've been. No dad. No money. Little kids at home. I made it. You will too. Let's go, brother. What flavor should we make?"

"How about chocolate," I said, laughing. "You know,

I'm starting to believe in wishes. I thought they could never come true, but now I see that they can, thanks to you."

Michael bought the stuff, and he, my sisters and I all had a great time making the cake. He came back later that night to have some. Mama brought some ice cream. She called Michael a Good Samaritan. I agreed. He sure helped me when I was in trouble. I'll never forget my eleventh birthday. It turned out to be one of my best.

A Discussion and Action Guide for Families

1. Why does Taylor start to steal a package of cupcakes, even though he knows it is wrong?
2. What do you think you would do if you didn't have enough money to have a special birthday celebration for someone in your family?
3. Why does Michael help Taylor?
4. Do you think Michael changes Taylor's life?
5. Why do you think this story is titled "Surprise!"?
6. Who has surprised you by helping you and maybe even loving you? Whom have you surprised in the same way?
7. Read and discuss the parable of the Good Samaritan in Luke 10:25-34. How can your family members become Good Samaritans? Whom can you help rather than ignore?

Jonathan's Family

It was Friday. School would be over in a few minutes. The children looked happy and excited at the thought of two whole days of free time to play and do whatever they wanted.

Everyone looked happy and excited except one boy, Jonathan Wainwright Sterling III. He didn't like weekends that much. It wasn't that he loved school, but on the weekends he never got to see his friends. Jonathan usually went out of the city to his family's country house. If his parents were away, he wasn't allowed to have anyone over or to go to a friend's house. That was their rule.

"See you all on Monday," Jonathan said, trying to force a smile, as he waved good-bye to his classmates.

Mrs. Doyle was waiting for him in front of the school, as she always was. She had been taking care of him since he was born, seven years ago. When he was younger, he used to get mixed up and call Mrs. Doyle "Mother." Now, of course, he knew better, but he still sometimes called her "Mother" to himself.

Mrs. Doyle smiled and patted him on the shoulder. "Well, Jonathan, my boy," she said. "How are you doing?"

"OK, I guess," Jonathan answered. "I got a hundred

on the spelling test. I finished my math. I just have some reading, and that's all."

"Oh, Jonathan," Mrs. Doyle said, "I wish my Kevin was as good at school as you are. He's a year older than you, but you're so far ahead of him."

Jonathan didn't know what to say. He had met Kevin only once, a long time ago. Kevin and his sister, Maureen, lived with their grandmother so that Mrs. Doyle could live with his family and take care of him. It didn't seem right, but Jonathan was very glad that she did.

"How about a treat, Jonathan?" Mrs. Doyle asked. "It feels like spring. How would an ice cream cone taste to you?"

"OK," Jonathan answered, adjusting his knapsack on his back. "I mean, thank you very much. I'd like that."

Jonathan knew that these treats came out of Mrs. Doyle's own money. His parents did not approve of sweets, but Mrs. Doyle saved them for special times, and his parents never really knew about them anyway. Sometimes Jonathan bought a treat for them both out of his allowance. It made him feel grown-up.

"Well, let's be going then," she said. "I want to see that face of yours full of smiles again."

"Me too," Jonathan answered.

As they walked down the street, Jonathan reached for her hand and held it tightly. Mrs. Doyle didn't ask him to talk. Jonathan loved that about her.

Jonathan ordered a chocolate cone, as he always did, and Mrs. Doyle had banana. She liked to try new things. They each took a taste of the other's cone, and both of them broke into smiles.

"I'm glad I got chocolate," Jonathan said.

"Bananas taste better on cereal," Mrs. Doyle agreed.

"Let's take a walk," Jonathan said. "I don't feel like going back to the apartment right now. With Mother and Father away, I won't get to see my friends again this weekend. I hate that rule of no friends when they aren't here! They don't know my friends anyway, not like you do."

Mrs. Doyle put her arm around him.

"I know it's hard," she said. "Your parents have been gone for almost two weeks, but they'll be back Monday night. Just be patient a bit longer, Jonathan."

Jonathan shrugged his shoulders and said, "I'll try."

They walked for almost an hour, stopping to look up at carved beasts and human faces on tall, tall buildings. Sometimes they ran races to street corners, starting when either of them would suddenly shout, "Go!"

Jonathan was feeling really happy by the time they got home. It seemed that all his blood was racing around his body, and his head felt so light that it might carry him away.

He felt that way until he walked into his bedroom to hang up his jacket. He had a large bedroom, with his own bathroom. Each of the walls had shelves for a different kind of thing. One wall was for board games and puzzles, another was for stuffed animals and toys, another was for books, and the fourth was for video games and his television. On his desk sat the latest present, which his parents had given him before they left on their cruise, a computer with a color monitor and a printer. Jonathan knew how to use it. He had plenty of the same software that he enjoyed using at school. But Jonathan hadn't even turned this computer on yet.

The room looked like a toy store, his parents always

said, the few times they ever came to his room. What his parents didn't know was that nobody plays with the toys in the store. They're just there to look at.

Whenever Jonathan was in his room, he remembered how lonely he was. Even if his parents bought him everything in the world, he still wouldn't have anyone to play with.

Jonathan ran out of the room and down to the kitchen,

where Mrs. Doyle was fixing dinner. As soon as he got there, he felt better.

"Can I help?" he asked. "Oh, I mean, may I help?"

Mrs. Doyle laughed.

"You can and you may," she said. "Why don't you set the table, and then you can cut these carrots. Just be careful that you don't cut your finger!"

"Aye, aye, Captain," Jonathan said, saluting.

"I'm glad for your help. Now get to work," she said.

"What are we having?" Jonathan asked.

"I made it for you," Mrs. Doyle said. "Take a guess."

"Is it Irish stew?" Jonathan asked.

"I can't ever surprise you!" she answered.

In a little while they were sitting down to large bowls of steaming, savory stew. Jonathan's carrots were bright boats of orange in a brown, mysterious ocean.

While they were talking and eating, Jonathan suddenly became very quiet, and started to play with his carrot boats, trying to make them sink.

Without looking up at Mrs. Doyle, he suddenly said, "Mrs. Doyle, do you ever get lonely, real lonely, like you're missing something, and then you get sad? You always look so happy. I wish I was."

Mrs. Doyle became very quiet herself. She also started to play with her stew. Then she looked up and smiled gently at Jonathan.

"Sure I do, Johnny," she said. "Everyone does, some time or another."

"But I feel that way all the time," Jonathan said. "I miss my parents, but even more, I wish I had a brother or maybe a sister. I'd even settle for some friends sleeping over. Don't you miss your family? Isn't it hard to see your children only on Sundays? And you haven't even done that the last two Sundays, all because of me."

"I miss them," Mrs. Doyle said. "I miss seeing them every day. I talk to them on the phone, but I miss seeing their faces. My mother takes good care of them, and they love her. That helps me. And Jonathan, you're like one of my own. You help me to be happy."

Jonathan got up from his place and went over, and Mrs. Doyle opened her arms and hugged him. Jonathan jumped up on her lap, as he used to do when he was little. It felt good to be there, safe and warm.

"Hey, I've got an idea," Jonathan slowly said. "A great idea!"

"Well, tell me. I can't wait!" Mrs. Doyle said.

"Let's you and me go stay at your house for the weekend. That way you can see your kids and I can play with them. Then we'll both be happy!" Jonathan exclaimed.

"Well, I don't think so," Mrs. Doyle said. "I'd have to ask your parents, and there's no way to reach them on that boat."

"Please, Mrs. Doyle, please, please," Jonathan begged. "Mother and Father wouldn't mind. They wouldn't even know. Come on."

"Now, Jonathan," Mrs. Doyle said. "Right is right. Don't beg me."

"It could be one of our little treats," Jonathan said.

"I'll think about it and tell you in the morning," Mrs. Doyle said. "Now let's clear the table, and then you can take your bath and get ready for bed. If we go, we'll get up early."

"Oh, thanks, Mrs. Doyle, you're super," Jonathan said.

"Don't thank me yet, young man," she said, "and start

clearing the table."

Jonathan was so excited that he could hardly sleep that night. When he woke up, he jumped out of bed, got dressed, and ran to the kitchen. What he saw made him grin.

"Mrs. Doyle," he said, "you've got on your going-home clothes. That's great!"

"Well, to tell you the truth," she said, "I'm not sure I'm doing the right thing. But when I talked to the children last night, it was clear they were really missing me, too. So I thought real hard, prayed and the sun came up, bright and beautiful, and said, 'Let's be going.'"

"Well, let's be going then," said Jonathan.

"After your breakfast, young man," she said. "It's about an hour by subway and bus. I think we'll just stay for the day, and come back tonight. I'd just feel better if I could tell your parents what we're doing."

"Don't worry," said Jonathan. "Remember, it was my idea."

"Eat your breakfast, now. Time's awasting," Mrs. Doyle said.

Jonathan put his pajamas, toothbrush and some clean clothes into his knapsack. He really wanted to spend the night, and he crossed his fingers as he thought about it.

Jonathan and Mrs. Doyle rode the subway to where it ended, and then they walked a few blocks to a bus stop. Jonathan had never been to this part of the city before. It was more like the country. The buildings weren't so tall, and you could see the sky.

"I like it here, Mrs. Doyle," Jonathan said. "I wish we

JESUS
LOVES
YOU

lived here. Look. There are kids running around everywhere."

"It is a friendly neighborhood," Mrs. Doyle said. "I miss it myself. Well, here we are. The next stop is ours. I hope I'm doing the right thing."

In a few minutes the two of them were walking up to the door of a small house. Two children and an older woman were on the porch waiting for them.

"Mommy, Mommy," the boy and girl yelled, jumping into her open arms.

Jonathan felt a little strange. He backed away and sighed.

The older woman said, "Hello, Jonathan. Welcome. We're so glad you came. We've heard so much about you. I'm Mrs. Doyle's mother, Mrs. Murphy."

"Thank you," Jonathan said. "It was my idea to come."

"And here are Kevin and Maureen," Mrs. Doyle said. "And this is Jonathan."

"Hi!" the children all said at once.

"Can we go play?" Kevin asked. "There's a ball game in the park. Joey and Patrick are already there."

Mrs. Doyle smiled. "I thought you were wanting to see me so bad! Well, be off with you. Just come home for lunch. We'll visit then."

"Mrs. Doyle," Jonathan asked, "may I go play too? I'll be careful."

"Of course, Jonathan," she answered. "That's why we came."

"Oh, boy," he said. "Oh, boy!"

The day went very fast. Jonathan couldn't remember ever having more fun. Kevin, Maureen and he ran back and forth all day, from the house to the park and all around the block. Mrs. Doyle seemed jollier than ever, and Mrs. Murphy was nice, too.

Of course they decided to spend the night. Kevin and Maureen had bunk beds in their room. Maureen usually slept in the lower bunk, but she said she would sleep on the couch so the boys could be together.

"I really like your room," Jonathan said to Kevin.

"It's nothing like yours," Kevin answered. "I've heard about all the stuff you have. I don't have much."

"You've got everything," Jonathan said.

After a minute or two more, both boys fell fast asleep.

When they woke up, it was Sunday morning. After a big breakfast, Mrs. Doyle said, "We always go to church on Sunday, Jonathan. We hope you'll come with us."

"Sure," Jonathan said. "We only go on Christmas and Easter. I always wondered what churches did the rest of the year."

"Well, you'll find out today," Mrs. Doyle said.

When they got to church, Jonathan was surprised that the building was so small, but then he realized that it was like everything else at Mrs. Doyle's, just the right size.

The people were friendly, and Jonathan liked the children's sermon about Jesus and the way he spent time with children. When the children left the sanctuary, they went to a big room with different activities to choose and do. Kevin and Jonathan decided to help paint a large mural, "The Church Serves Others." Before they knew it, it was noon and time to go.

"I like your church," Jonathan said as they were walking home. "I wish I could go every Sunday."

"You can!" Kevin and Maureen exclaimed together.

Mrs. Doyle smiled but didn't say anything.

When they walked into the house, the phone was ringing. Maureen rushed to answer it.

"It's for you, Mom," she said.

"Hello?" Mrs. Doyle said, her face becoming pale as she spoke.

"Yes, Mr. Sterling," she said. "He's here. With me. He's fine. I'm sorry. I didn't know how to reach you. I didn't think. Yes. We'll be back at the apartment this afternoon. You're staying an extra three days? Home Thursday. Fine, Mr. Sterling. Would you like to talk to Jonathan? Here he is. Good-bye, sir."

"Hello, Father," Jonathan said. "Coming here was all my idea. I talked Mrs. Doyle into it. Really. I had a great time. There's kids to play with all day long, and we went to a neat church. I'm fine, Father. I miss you and Mother, too. See you tomorrow. Oh, Thursday? OK. Good-bye."

Jonathan hung up the phone. He blinked twice and tried to smile. It was hard.

"I'm sorry I got you in trouble, Mrs. Doyle," Jonathan said.

"It's all right," she said. "Seeing you and Kevin and Maureen play together has been a joy. I hope we can all be together again. But we'll be sure to ask next time!"

"Everyone can come to our apartment next time," Jonathan said. "I'd love that!"

Jonathan reached up and gave Mrs. Doyle a hug. Kevin and Maureen joined in and made Jonathan feel even better. Two families were better than one.

A Discussion and Action Guide for Families

1. Why didn't Jonathan play with his toys? What did he want more than toys?
2. When was he most happy?
3. What makes you sad? What makes you happy?
4. What does your family enjoy doing together? What new things would you like to try?
5. Who would you like to invite to join you?
6. Read the story of the rich young man in Matthew 19:16-22. If people choose to follow Jesus, what will they choose to do about money?
7. In what way is Mrs. Doyle's family richer than Jonathan's family? Do you think Jonathan will care about others when he grows up? Why?

Gifts Shared

My dad loves fishing. He should—he's a fisherman. He has his own boat, which is named after me, Claudia. When I don't have school, I like to go out fishing with him. He likes my company and my help, too. When the fishing was better, Dad would always have a teenager who had finished school on board with him. The work was safer and faster that way. But now the fishing's not so good, and we can't afford to pay anyone. The teenagers would like to help us out, but their families need money too, and they can't work for nothing.

I don't know where all the fish went. They're probably gone because of a lot of things, like too many boats, especially those huge ones that are really floating factories. Our boat looks like a rowboat next to them. It seems the fish have moved further off the coast, and it takes more and more time and gasoline to go and find them.

We've been fishing all our lives—both of my grandfathers had boats. When they first came here, almost everyone fished. It must have been fun. I wish I could have seen it. I wouldn't want to have lived then, though. Girls never went on the boats. They mainly helped at home. I like to do both.

My dad's a good man. He loves almost everything and everyone. "We're all children of the same God," he always says. He has taught me a lot, about the sea, animals, nature and people, too. He hardly ever gets upset. That's why I got worried last night.

Dad was sitting at the kitchen table, working on his bills. He was figuring how much money he had made fishing and how much he owed other people, for fishing expenses and for our family. He must have been working for an hour or more. Finally, he just folded his arms on top of the papers and put his head down.

"I don't know what to do," he said. "I just don't know. There aren't enough fish. There's not enough money. Maybe we should sell the boat."

"Next week or next month will be better," Mama said, putting her hand on his back. "I can get more houses to clean. I'll just work a little faster, that's all."

"You can have my allowance, Daddy. I haven't spent all of it. That will help," I said.

Dad looked up. He was almost smiling again. "Thanks, Claudia," he said. "I don't think we'll need *all* your allowance. And thanks, Jeanne, but I hope it doesn't come to that. I'd not want to see you having to work in other people's houses any more than you already do. But it's good of you two to remind me that we're rowing our boat together. Sometimes it's hard to remember that all our days come from the Creator, the stormy days and the clear ones. And it's our job to make the best of what we're given. So there's no point in worrying any more tonight about these pieces of paper. I'm going down to my workshop and whittle a bit. Anybody care to join me?"

"I can't," Mama said. "I've got six pies to make for the church fair tomorrow."

"Why don't you make seven? The extra one can be for us," Dad said.

"I was counting on it," Mama answered.

"I'll come down with you," I said. "I want to work on my bird."

"What kind is it?" Dad asked.

"I'm not sure yet," I answered.

"I'll help you," he said. "You can always turn it into a Canadian goose."

I laughed and said, "Right."

Dad's a wonderful wood carver. Sometimes I think he loves carving more than fishing. Or maybe he loves them both the same.

He makes beautiful little boats and big ships. He carves seals and walrus, whales, and all kinds of birds. My favorites are his imaginary creatures from the bottom of the sea. Each one is very different.

As I looked around the workroom shelves, which were filled with carvings, I suddenly had an idea.

"Dad," I said, "do you think I could take some of your carvings up to the church fair? We've got so many, and we could sell some. We keep part of the money, and the church keeps part."

"Sure, do what you want, Claudia," Dad said. "I think you'll be wasting your time, but that's what I do every day, too. Take as many as you want. That way I'll have room to make more."

"What should I charge?" I asked.

"Not much," Dad answered. "How about ten cents for small, thirty cents for medium and fifty cents for large?"

"That's not enough, Dad," I answered. "I'll charge one dollar, three dollars, and five dollars."

"You'll never sell a one at those prices," Dad said.

"Wait and see," I said. "Don't forget people who are on vacation."

"Maybe you're right," Dad answered. "How many do you want to take?"

"I'll take about twenty-five. That should do it," I said.

I picked out my favorite animals from the workshop shelves. (Of course, my most favorite ones were already in my bedroom.) I took five big ones—sea creatures, ships and a seal—and ten medium and ten small—a combination of birds, seals and whales. I dusted each of them and shined them up. They looked great. Instead of putting price tags on each animal, I decided to make one sign for each size. That would be simpler and could wait until morning. Right now I was ready to have a piece of pie, read a little bit and go to bed. The way I figured it, if everything sold, we'd make sixty-five dollars. Wow!

I woke up a bit late the next morning, so I had to rush. I didn't have time to make the signs at home, but I took paper and markers with me. I took an old card table along too, so I could fix up a real nice display.

"Good luck," Dad said, as Mama and I drove away. "I'll be there in a little while."

I found a shady spot, where I'd be comfortable for the day, and Mama went inside to where the food was being sold.

I set up the animals and had just finished the price signs when a woman rushed past me to look at my table. She picked up the different animals and looked carefully at each, first with her glasses on, then with them off. She

even smelled them. I didn't know if she thought they were alive or what.

"Did you make these?" she asked.

"Oh, no, my dad did," I answered.

"I'll take them," she said.

"Which one?" I asked.

"I'll take them all," she said.

"Why?" I asked.

"I have a shop in the city. They'll sell very well there. Your prices are reasonable, so I'll still make my profit. Would you take a check? I don't have that much cash."

"Sure," I answered. "I'll wrap them up for you."

After I wrapped them, she handed me the check. I gulped.

"This isn't right," I said.

"Well, your sign reads, '$50.00 for large, $30.00 for medium, and $10.00 for small.' That's six hundred and fifty dollars for the twenty-five animals," she said.

"I made a mistake. I'm not good at decimals. This is too much," I said.

"Never mind," she said, smiling now. "These are marvelous examples of folk art. Here's my card. When your father has some more, have him call me. I think we can do business together."

"Would you like to meet him?" I asked.

"Not now, dear," she said. "I've got to dash. I'm doing all the fairs today."

Before I knew it, she was gone, and there I was with my empty table and funny signs.

I walked over to the food booth, and Dad was already there.

"Hi, Claudia," he said. "I hope you're not discouraged so soon. It will take you all day to sell one or two of those carvings."

"Dad," I said, "I sold them all—to one lady."

"No!" Dad said. "I can't believe it. That's really something. What's she going to do with them all? Maybe she needed kindling."

"And Dad," I said, "I made a mistake on the prices.

I charged too much. But she didn't care. She said she would sell them in her shop for more than what she paid. Here's the check. She made it out to you. I had your name on the sign."

I handed Dad the check. I had never seen his eyes get that big before.

"Six hundred and fifty dollars!" he said. "Now I really can't believe it. That woman must be crazy."

"She said your carvings were something called folk art, and that she would buy more. Here's her card," I said.

"I guess it's real," Dad said. "I still can't believe it. Last night I was so worried, and now this. We'll give half to the church, and the other half will help pay our bills. Thanks, Claudia. This really saves us, for a while anyway."

"Maybe I won't take extra cleaning jobs," Mama said. "I can help with the carvings."

"Great," Dad answered. "You know, I could teach the children in the church how to carve, as a way to thank God and the church for the blessings of this day."

"That would be fun, Dad," I said.

"And we'll be sharing our gifts," Mama said. "Gifts shared are like loaves and fishes. They multiply and feed many."

We hugged each other and then got to work making sandwiches and cutting the pies. It was almost lunch time, and the people would be hungry.

Dad began to whistle. It was good to see him be his cheerful self again. Mama and I started whistling too.

A Discussion and Action Guide for Families

1. What gifts does each person in the story have?
2. How do the father, mother and daughter help each other?
3. What gifts does each person in your family have?
4. How do members of your family help one another?
5. How important is God to this family? How can you tell?
6. How important is God to your family? How can you tell?
7. Read about Jesus feeding more than four thousand people in Matthew 15:32-39. What miracle happens when a little food is blessed and shared? Does your family develop and share its special gifts? What happens when you do?

Answered Prayer

I am a newcomer to North America. My two children and I have lived here less than one year. In my own country, Cambodia, there was much war, much hunger, much sickness. My wife died before we left. We miss her very much. Life is not easy.

Yet I am very grateful to be in North America for all the freedoms. It is especially good not to be so afraid of the police and other people in authority. I am glad every day when I wake up and every night when I go to sleep. I am trying always to thank God for our many blessings. Then I ask for God's help with our problems.

I have a job working in a small grocery store. I have long hours, but I make more money than I ever could in my country. The owners of the store like me, and I get to take some food home for my children. It is free. It is like a miracle to me.

The big problem I have is what to do with my children now that it is summer. They have no school, and it is hard for me to leave them in our room alone all day when I go to work. I wish they could come with me, but it is not allowed.

I have a boy, Phuon Rom, who is eight, and a girl,

Mam Rom, who is seven. They are good children, but I worry for them to be inside all day, but to be outside on the street is not good either.

We used to live in a nice apartment with separate rooms for cooking and sleeping. There were people who helped me with my children. They were like uncles, aunts or grandparents. Then that building was sold, and we all had to leave. I had no place to go, not enough money for a new good home. Not yet. So the city found a place for us. It is OK, but not such a good place. The people seem more frightened. They are not so friendly. Some seem to be selling drugs or doing other bad things. They turn away when we walk by them.

I hope to move out, but what can I do with my children now? I want to stay with them. But if I do not go to work, we cannot pay to move. I think and wait and pray, but no answer comes to me.

Finally something happens. I am walking through the lobby with my children. I notice a woman that I have seen before sitting there. She always looks at us and nods her head. Sometimes she smiles. She is an older woman and seems to have peace within her.

I decide all at once to approach her, even though I am not certain it is right to do so.

"Excuse me," I say. "May I have a moment to speak with you?"

"Certainly," she says. "I have seen you and your sweet children many times. I should have introduced myself. I'm Beverly Jones."

"I am Sarin Rom. These are my children, Phuon and Mam. Their mother, unfortunately, has died in Cambodia."

"Hello, children. I'm happy to meet you. I am sorry

about your mother, very sorry," Mrs. Jones says.

"I need to find out, Mrs. Jones, what I can do for my children this summer while I am at work. Leaving them here alone is not good. They cannot go with me. Yet

I must work so we can live. Do you have any idea? I do regret asking you to spend your time on my problem."

"Nonsense," says Mrs. Jones. "God put us here to help one another. That's what the Good Book, the Bible, says. Let's see. What days do you work?"

"I work all days. I must," I say.

"Well, I think you need a day of rest. Even God got one of those, you know," she says. "But that's your business. I know it's hard supporting two children, especially when you're alone. I did it myself. Now look where I live. But I expect to be moving soon."

"I was wondering about some days, not all days," I say. "I would like the children to be able to run and play outside. I do not want them only indoors. It's not good. It's not right."

"Well, I may have the perfect solution," Mrs. Jones says. "It could solve your problem."

"I would be most pleased if you would tell me," I say.

"My church runs a camp in the summer. It's about an hour's ride out of the city. The kids leave at eight o'clock in the morning and return about six in the evening. There are swimming, boating, games and, of course, Bible study and worship every day. Lunch is included too."

Phuon and Mam start jumping up and down. Their faces are all smiles.

"Be still, my children," I say. "We could never pay for such a camp. We only have money for our room and our food. Thank you, Mrs. Jones, your thought was a beautiful one. Now we will go, and trouble you no longer. Thank you for your time."

"Why, Mr. Rom, you didn't let me finish," Mrs. Jones

says. "At our church camp, the families pay what they can afford. Some pay much, some pay little."

"But how can this be?" I ask. "Who pays for food and teachers and boats and everything else?"

"Our church pays most of the expenses," Mrs. Jones says. "We remember Jesus saying that when you help the needy, you are helping him. All kids need to go to camp—especially city kids."

"But we are not members of your church," I say. "Would we be welcome?"

"The camp was started about one hundred years ago, so that city children could get fresh air and exercise while getting to know God in the beauty of nature," Mrs. Jones answers. "Of course you would be welcome to come to church and join the church, but it's not required or even expected."

"This is too wonderful," I say. "I am afraid I dream and will awake. What must I do to see if they will take my children?"

"I'll go call the minister," Mrs. Jones says. "I'm sure there's room. We were just saying yesterday that there were some spaces we hoped to fill. I'm so glad you spoke with me. Wait a minute. I'll use the pay phone and let you know right away."

While Mrs. Jones is phoning, I put my arms around my children, waiting in silence, hoping and praying there will be room for them at the camp.

Mrs. Jones comes back smiling.

"If you would like," she says, "I can take you to the church office now, and the children can start tomorrow. No point in waiting around and wasting time, right?"

"Of course we will go now," I say. "Our prayers have

been answered. Thank you, Mrs. Jones."

"Thank you, Mr. Rom. Your children will be fine additions to our camp. I can see that."

The next day, when I go to work, I take the children to the church. A big yellow bus is waiting and filled with noisy children.

Phuon and Mam hold on to me, and do not want to get on the bus. I am afraid that they will not go, and my problem of how to care for them will remain.

Then a lovely young woman steps off the bus.

"Hello, Phuon. Hello, Mam. I'm Amy, a counselor. I'll help you find a seat and your first new friend. OK?"

She reaches out a hand to each of them. They take her hands and, turning to wave good-bye, get onto the bus. They seem to be smiling as the bus pulls away, but I cannot be sure. The bus moves too quickly.

This day at work seems like it will never end. I keep looking at the clock. Finally it is time for me to go meet the children at church.

The bus is late and I walk around nervously waiting for it. Then it comes. The bus seems alive with singing and shouts of joy.

Phuon and Mam are the first off the bus. Both of them are holding hands with other children. They all come running up to me.

"Papa, Papa," Mam says, "the camp is the most beautiful place in North America—a blue lake, green mountains, and golden fields."

"It is fun there all day," Phuon says. "We swam, played ball and worshiped God—when we first got there, and right before we left to come back home. This is Sam, my best friend."

CAMPBUS
CAMP

"And this is Judy, she's my friend," Mam says.

"I am honored to meet you both," I say. "We will see you tomorrow."

"See you tomorrow," the children yell together. Phuon and Mam never stop talking all the way home. I cannot stop smiling as I listen to their happy voices.

A Discussion and Action Guide for Families

1. Ask each member of your family what they like best about the summer. Make a list of indoor and outdoor activities. Make plans to do some of the things each person likes to do.

2. What would your family do if you faced the problem of the father in the story? Would camp be a way to solve the problem for you? What else might you do?

3. Does your church or denomination have a summer camp? Get information on it to share. See if the children in your family are interested in camp. Encourage other families to do the same. Is your camp only for church members or may others attend? Try to find out. If camperships or sliding scale payments are not available, try to see if money can be raised to help needy children attend the camp.

4. Tell one another about your memorable outdoor experiences, whether in a city park or in a rustic camp. Include those experiences that have affected your faith in God.

5. Read and discuss Matthew 25:31-46. This is the passage Mrs. Jones mentions in the story. In the passage, Jesus says that when we help others we are also helping him. Think of those who have helped you and those who need your help. Choose a practical way to assist one or more persons who need your help. Some refugees who have moved to the area where you live might need your assistance.

ESCAPING THE DARKNESS OF MY HEART

Donated in Honor of
Kendra J Williams
By
Jackie Williams